Sarah's Garden

Amy Dawn Belcourt

AuthorHouse™
1663 Liberty Drive
Bloomington, IN 47403
www.authorhouse.com
Phone: 1 (800) 839-8640

Published by AuthorHouse: 7/22/2015

ISBN: 978-1-5049-2448-1 (sc)
ISBN: 978-1-5049-2449-8 (e)

Library of Congress Control Number: 2015911714

Print information available on the last page.

authorHOUSE®

My sister woke up one day, she couldn't go to school, and she couldn't play.
We all stayed home and had a cozy day together. That is What we usually did with mommy when we felt under the weather.

Sarah smiled, and she laughed at me, she giggled at our baby Brother Jeffrey. All day we watched movies, we cuddled with mom and Dad, we sat together on the couch then Sarah's headache started to Get very bad.

We got out the blankets and snuggled next to mom, my big sisters Breath was slow and soon gone. We had to go to the hospital, we wanted her to open her eyes. No one would expect that my sister would Die. I asked mommy what happened. She did not even understand. When will Sarah come back? I wanted my big sister, my Best friend.

Was this real? Was it a dream?

Family gathered around us, and friends from everywhere to give us all Hugs as Sarah leaving us was not at all fair. I got to see my Aunties, Uncles, Cousins, Grandma and Grandpa! We had a Funeral to say our goodbyes. I see mommy and daddy with tears all the time. I know it hurts their hearts as it also hurts mine. Why did this happen? Sarah was not sick the day before she left us?

My sister had a brain Aneurysm; I don't really know what that is. It Happened so very fast. It is not fair, she was only a kid.

I felt very angry, very sad…. Everyone tells me that it is hard on our feelings when somebody we love dies. They are gone but never forgotten. That everyday will hurt, but it does get easier.

We have lots of pictures and belongings of Sarah's that we look at every day.

We planted a garden with flowers all around, with stones and Decorations that we lay on the ground. We have charms on the fence and sun catchers in the trees, streamers and balloons that blow beautifully in the breeze.

Others close to us have brought things to place there as well.

I like to go in my back yard to see what has grown over night. I see Purple, yellow, green and pink and I Count the new sprouts 1,2 and 3!

I love to sing and dance, that is what I miss a lot about my Sister. I Like to pretend she is hiding in the garden, or I look for her in the Sky. I laugh at her, but sometimes I cry. It is okay to cry. I learned about feelings at daycare and school. When you are sad you can cry, when you are happy you laugh and smile and when I am mad I will scream. I am sad and mad that Sarah is gone. I am happy when I think of all the fun things we did together.

Sarah's Garden is very beautiful, full of colors and love. Sarah is An angel now....and I believe she always was.

To a very dear family...

I still cannot express the sadness I feel in my heart for you every day. I see the posts and pictures of the beautiful garden and how much work and effort has been put in to making it perfect. I wanted to write a children's book for other children and families to understand that no matter what age we are, the unthinkable can happen. Life is real and unfair at times, but tragic loss does exist and together we need to support those around us who have experienced this great pain as you have. I love you all.

Angel up in heaven, you are so very loved.

About Brain Aneurysms

The medical term for an aneurysm that develops inside the brain is an intracranial or cerebral aneurysm.

Most brain aneurysms will only cause noticeable symptoms if they burst or rupture.

This will lead to an extremely serious condition, where bleeding caused by the ruptured aneurysm can cause extensive brain damage and symptoms such as:

- a sudden agonizing headache – it has been described as a 'thunderclap headache', similar to a sudden hit on the head, resulting in a blinding pain unlike anything experienced before
- stiff neck
- sickness and vomiting
- pain from looking at light
- If one pupil looks larger than the other

If you notice these symptoms in yourself or anyone else, please do not hesitate to contact your doctor or go to Emergency facility right away.

CPSIA information can be obtained
at www.ICGtesting.com
Printed in the USA
LVOW05s1956261015

459849LV00016B/83/P